T0210005

Be a farmer for God

NICK DENVER

Copyright © 2020 Nick Denver.

All rights reserved. No part of this book may be used or reproduced by any means, graphic, electronic, or mechanical, including photocopying, recording, taping or by any information storage retrieval system without the written permission of the author except in the case of brief quotations embodied in critical articles and reviews.

This book is a work of non-fiction. Unless otherwise noted, the author and the publisher make no explicit guarantees as to the accuracy of the information contained in this book and in some cases, names of people and places have been altered to protect their privacy.

WestBow Press books may be ordered through booksellers or by contacting:

WestBow Press
A Division of Thomas Nelson & Zondervan
1663 Liberty Drive
Bloomington, IN 47403
www.westbowpress.com
844-714-3454

Because of the dynamic nature of the Internet, any web addresses or links contained in this book may have changed since publication and may no longer be valid. The views expressed in this work are solely those of the author and do not necessarily reflect the views of the publisher, and the publisher hereby disclaims any responsibility for them.

Scriptures taken from the Holy Bible, New International Version®, NIV®. Copyright © 1973, 1978, 1984, 2011 by Biblica, Inc.™ Used by permission of Zondervan. All rights reserved worldwide. www.zondervan.com The "NIV" and "New International Version" are trademarks registered in the United States Patent and Trademark Office by Biblica, Inc.®

Any people depicted in stock imagery provided by Getty Images are models, and such images are being used for illustrative purposes only. Certain stock imagery © Getty Images.

ISBN: 978-1-6642-1473-6 (sc)
ISBN: 978-1-6642-1475-0 (hc)
ISBN: 978-1-6642-1474-3 (e)

Library of Congress Control Number: 2020923684

Print information available on the last page.

WestBow Press rev. date: 12/10/2020

WESTBOW
PRESS®
A DIVISION OF THOMAS NELSON
& ZONDERVAN

Be a farmer for God

Hi, my name is Matt and I want to tell you how you can be a farmer for God.

"A farmer for God? What does that mean?" you may ask.

Ok, let's start with a farmer and what he does: A farmer sows seeds and waters them, over time something grows from the seeds and once it is full grown he harvests what he had sown.

Now you and I can do the same for God by telling our friends, who have never heard of Jesus, that he died on the cross for all people!

We can be like the farmer to plant a seed in the people we tell about Jesus, and one day God will reap what we had sown when they believe in Jesus Christ as their saviour.

Here is Jesus' story:

God's plan was to send Jesus to earth as a human being to live among the people and die for them, but rise again so that all of us can have a right relationship with God and go to heaven when we die.

This is true, because it is in the bible and God wrote the bible through all the authors who he himself had inspired.

Here is what it says in the book of Mark: "Go into all the world and preach the gospel to all creation." — MARK 16:15, NIV

God wants us to tell everyone about him, because he loves all of us so much! Isn't that great?

This is how to be a farmer for God!

Now you may ask, how you can do that:

You can invite everybody from your class or sports team or co-curricular club to come to church with you on Sunday. That's what I did with my friend Jeff. Jeff was new to our school and since the beginning of the school year we had been sitting beside each other.

One Friday I asked him, if he wanted to join my family and me to go to church the coming Sunday. He said that he didn't know and that he had to talk to his parents first. They said: "Ok." So we went to Sunday school that Sunday and he had a good time. He said that he might be back some day. Weeks later I asked him again, and he joined in. This went on for months and Jeff heard and learned more and more about Jesus.

Try the same, but don't be disappointed if people don't want to come, just keep on trying!

In the book of John we read the most popular verse in the bible: "For God so loved the world that he gave his one and only son, that whoever believes in him shall not perish, but have eternal life." —- JOHN 3:16, NIV

God loves everyone and that's why we need to tell everyone, because God wants them all to go to heaven and be with him forever.

We can all have a relationship with God by believing in him and by talking to him in prayer. We can ask God for help through prayer:

If someone at school has been mean to you and has said mean things, you can pray and forgive this person.

Give thanks for your friends and all the things that have happened to you this day (good or bad).

Thank him for all the stuff you have or pray for healing if you or someone in your family or someone else is sick.

I said this prayer when my little sister had the flu: "Father God, my sister has had a nasty flu for the past five days, she has a high fever. Please heal her! It really bothers her and it bothers me seeing her lying in bed. In Jesus name I pray! Amen!"

One day I did one of my chores at home. It was spring time and so it was time to plant some seeds for the new season. The neighbour's daughter Olivia, who is my age, saw me working and came over asking if she could help. Great idea, I thought, so we both dug the holes, put the seeds in and closed them again. About 22 of them.

A verse from the bible, which my dad had read to me the night before came to my mind:

"The one who sowed the good seed is the Son of Man. The field is the world and the good seed stands for the sons of the kingdom." MATTHEW 13:37, NIV

That means that when we believe in Jesus Christ, we should continue the good work for God by telling everybody in the world about him. That's what I said to Olivia and I thanked her for helping me.

I play hockey on a team, we practice twice a week and it is big fun. The kids on my team are from all over the place which means that not all of us live in the same neighbourhood. One guy named Danny lives about an hour away, his parents don't mind the drive to practice and he is nice. After getting to know him better I found out that he goes to church on Sundays and that his family believes in Jesus Christ. So I asked him if he had tried to invite people from his class or other activities to church. And he said, yes. He said that he had invited these twin brothers from his class to his Sunday school and they wanted to come every Sunday ever since. He said that they really liked the candy which they hand out, but everything else, the crafts and the games and activities they play was what they really enjoyed. The biggest part of it though, for these twins was, that everybody in church gets a chance. It does not matter how good, fast or smart you are, everybody is the same.

I really liked Danny's story and it helped me to continue to tell kids about Jesus. In MATTHEW 5:16, NIV Jesus says: "In the same way, let your light shine before others, that they may see your good deeds and glorify your Father in heaven."

Here is another really cool story from the bible. David and Goliath from 1 SAMUEL 17:45, NIV. You may have heard about it already: Here are these two tribes called the Israelites and the Philistines at war and they have gathered their armies on a hill each, there is a valley in between them. From the Philistines there is a giant soldier named Goliath and he comes out every morning to mock the Israelites, who will fight him. If the Israelites win, the Philistines will become their slaves, if the Philistines win, the Israelites will become their slaves, he says. This had been going on for a long time. Until one day a shepherd boy named David said that he will fight the giant. He had God on his side, he said, because he had killed a bear and a lion, which had tried to steal some of his sheep earlier. He had a sling shot and some stones with him. When they tried to put armour on him it did not fit, because it was too big. So he went just the way he was.

He said to Goliath: " You come against me with sword, spear and javelin, but I come against you in the name of the Lord Almighty, the God of the armies of Israel, whom you have defied!" So, when the giant approached him, he put a stone in his sling shot and shot it into Goliath's face. The giant fell face down, when the Philistines saw this they ran away.

Now, the reason why I think that this is a cool story is, because it can help you and me to become an everyday hero. We can be David when we face problems that seem to be too big for us. If, for example, another kid is mean to you, you can stand up against them, because you can trust that God will be with you and that he will strengthen you and give you the courage to tell your parents or teacher.

Be a blessing to others by being a farmer for God!

Printed in the United States
By Bookmasters